Original title:
Geranium Gems

Copyright © 2025 Creative Arts Management OÜ
All rights reserved.

Author: Liam Sterling
ISBN HARDBACK: 978-1-80566-747-6
ISBN PAPERBACK: 978-1-80566-817-6

Fragments of Colorful Joy

In pots of laughter, colors bloom,
Bright reds and pinks, they dispel the gloom.
With a dance in the breeze, they sway so spry,
Whispering jokes as the bees buzz by.

Their leaves are laughing, a playful green,
Each petal a wink, a cheeky scene.
They tickle the sun with their vibrant show,
A festival of hues, oh what a glow!

Cradled in Petals

A cozy nest where blooms reside,
Soft petals cradle, they cannot hide.
Tiny critters peek out with glee,
In this fluffy world, they're wild and free.

A ladybug wears a tiny cap,
Tea parties held in a dainty lap.
In laughter woven, their stories unfold,
In this petal palace, joy's manifold.

Elysium of the Earth

Bright colors tossed in the charming air,
Dancing on stems, without a care.
They giggle and shimmer in playful strife,
As if flowers know the magic of life.

A bumblebee comes, with a drumming beat,
In this earth-bound paradise, oh so sweet.
They jest and tease, nature's silly jest,
In this riot of colors, we're truly blessed.

Spirit of the Sun-Kissed

Basking in sunbeams, a merry crew,
Colors collide in a jolly hue.
Each bloom a burst, a chuckle so bright,
Life's little jokes, under warm daylight.

They tickle the clouds with their vibrant cheer,
Each petal a giggle, a hug so near.
In this sunny patch where joy takes flight,
Every glance at them fills the heart with light.

A Symphony of Blooms

In a pot, a dance begins,
Leaves wave like tiny fins,
Colors clash, oh what a sight,
Bumbling bees join in the light.

Silly petals in a row,
Strut their stuff and steal the show,
A trumpet bloom, a tuba sprout,
Making music, roundabout.

Blossoms of Enchantment

Once a flower thought it wise,
To wear shoes and don a tie,
Waltzing with a bumblebee,
"Oh darling, dance along with me!"

Petal hats and fragrant gowns,
Swirling 'round, they twirl in towns,
Frogs are croaking, what a scene,
They join in steps—our garden's queen!

Petal-Pusher's Delight

A petal tries to hitch a ride,
On a snail, oh, what a slide!
"Faster, dear!" it shouts with glee,
"Let's zoom past that big old tree!"

The dandelions laugh and tease,
As the leaves catch the summer breeze,
Racing roots and stems collide,
What a merry, joyful ride!

Hidden in the Garden

Behind the hedge, a secret crew,
Of squishy bugs and ants askew,
They plot and scheme, oh such a thrill,
Planning how to raid the dill!

A flower peeks, it laughs out loud,
As worms parade, they form a crowd,
Today's the day, they say with cheer,
To conquer veggies and spread good cheer!

Scarlets Beneath Twilight

In a garden where the night birds sing,
Red petals giggle, is it spring?
Swaying lightly, they dance around,
In a riot, petals all astound.

Beneath the stars, they whisper bold,
Tales of mischief, never told.
With nectar sweet, they plot and scheme,
Turning twilight into a dream.

Nature's Artisan: Stroke by Stroke

With each brushstroke, colors tease,
Artists ponder, won't they freeze?
Swirls of red and leafy green,
Nature's craft, a comical scene.

Pollen flies like little pranks,
In this garden, laughter tanks.
Petals paint on the morning's dew,
Making faces, just for you.

Lush Soliloquies of the Leafy Realm

In leafy halls where whispers bloom,
Every plant claims space and room.
Sassy stems with stories rife,
Claiming they lead a blooming life.

Frogs croak in agreement, bold,
As flowers tell of gossip, old.
Laughter sprouts from every nook,
In this vivid, silly book.

Embrace of the Brilliant Flora

In a glitch of colors so divine,
These floral jesters frolic, shine.
With petals flailing, bold and bright,
They charm the moon to take a bite.

Cactus sneers, "I'm spiky chic!"
While daisies giggle, hide and peek.
In this embrace, the blooms unite,
Crafting laughter, pure delight.

Nature's Crimson Symphony

In gardens bright, they strut with flair,
Tiny petals prance in the air.
Whispers giggle on the breeze,
As colors clash like playful tease.

With leaves that wave like tiny hands,
Each bloom has dreams of rockstar bands.
They shimmy in the warming sun,
And laugh aloud, it's all in fun.

A ladybug joins the silly show,
With polka dots, a dazzling glow.
They cheer for bees that buzz around,
In this floral circus, joy is found.

So raise a cup, let laughter bloom,
In this garden, there's no room for gloom.
With nature's jesters on parade,
Life's riotous colors never fade.

Blooms of Heavenly Delight

A splash of red in morning light,
These blossoms make the world feel right.
With cheeky grins and petals bright,
They dance with clouds, a silly sight.

The sun shines down with a wink and grin,
While bumblebees hum a tune within.
Petals tease the breeze that blows,
Swaying like they're in a show.

Roots take hold beneath the fun,
While squirrels plot to join their run.
Each flower bursts in laughter's call,
With petals painted, standing tall.

In this arena of vibrant play,
Nature's laughter leads the way.
So come and join this merry sight,
Where blooms share joy, pure and bright.

The Language of Blooming Hearts

In shades of red, the petals speak,
A language bold, though soft and sleek.
They jest and jive in sunny glee,
Sprouting smiles for all to see.

Each blossom's tale is rich and bright,
Like secret whispers in the night.
A cheeky bud with tales to tell,
Of garden dreams, where laughter swells.

They giggle as the raindrops fall,
Glorious blooms, now standing tall.
With every breeze, a chuckle shared,
In nature's playground, none is scared.

So let your heart find joy anew,
In every color, every hue.
For blooms and hearts are quite the team,
Creating laughter, living the dream.

A Dance of Scarlet Elegance

With twirls and swirls, they take the stage,
Each bud a star, they seize the age.
A flirty bow, a bold ballet,
In nature's dance, they laugh and sway.

The wind joins in with playful spins,
A flowered fiesta where glee begins.
With petals cascading like a gown,
They jive with joy, they spin around.

As butterflies swoop in to play,
The garden buzzes, hip-hip-hooray!
A symphony of colors bright,
In every twist, they shine with light.

So lift your spirits, join the fun,
With twinkling blooms, get ready to run.
In this garden dance, none can resist,
For laughter blooms, it can't be missed.

Mystique of the Petals

A flower once wore a silly hat,
It danced around, just like a cat.
The bees all giggled, they couldn't believe,
A bloom so bright, it made them weave.

In the garden, laughter echoed wide,
Petals pranced, twirling side to side.
A butterfly swooped down to say,
"What a party! Let's join the play!"

With colors bold and fragrance sweet,
They jived to a tune, a fragrant beat.
The sun peeked down with a wink and grin,
A playful day, where all could spin.

So if you spy a flower with flair,
Join the fun, just stop and stare.
For in that moment, pure delight,
A garden of joy, oh, what a sight!

Enchanted Bloomers

In the garden where the laughter grows,
Each petal wears a pair of shoes.
They twinkle, sparkle, and sometimes fight,
Who dances best in the morning light?

A rose claimed she could do the twist,
A daisy giggled, 'You've got me missed!'
Beneath the leaves, they took a chance,
With roots that tapped, they began to prance.

"Oh look!" cried Lily, "I can moonwalk!"
The daisies chuckled, "Now that's just talk!"
But as they jived through the sunny air,
They discovered joy was everywhere.

So gather 'round, let's celebrate,
The flowers' dance, oh, isn't it great?
With laughter pure and colors bright,
Their enchanted bloomers bring delight!

Beneath the Canopy

Under the trees where shadows play,
A flower whispered, "Let's have a say!"
"Who's got the best joke in this patch?
Let's see who can make the gnarled roots hatch!"

A tulip chimed in, "Knock knock, my friend!"
"Who's there?" said Fern, on that they depend.
"Leaf!" laughed Tulip, "Leaf me alone!"
But laughter erupted like seeds overthrown.

A daffodil blurted, "I can rhyme!"
Everyone giggled, "Oh, that's just prime!"
The daisies summoned a pun on a breeze,
Their jokes were sprouting like buzzing bees.

So beneath the leafy, shady dome,
The flowers found their fun-filled home.
With every quip and playful jest,
Life in the garden was truly the best!

Melodies of the Flora

In a garden where blooms serenade,
The flowers formed a cheeky brigade.
"Let's sing a song," a poppy exclaimed,
"And charm the bees with tunes unframed!"

A daisy piped up, a bit off-key,
But in that moment, it felt so free.
"With petals for instruments, we'll create,
A harmony that'll shake the gate!"

The violets clapped their leafy hands,
As daisies tapped out quirky bands.
"Plant a seed of joy," cheered a bold rose,
"Together we dance, in vibrant prose!"

So let us sing, let our petals sway,
In this funny garden where fun won't stray.
For beneath the sun, with laughter so pure,
The melodies of flora will always endure!

Echoes of the Garden

In the plot where daisies play,
A loud bee buzzed the day away.
He tried to sing, but lost his tune,
While flirting hard with a big balloon.

Worms in hats parade with glee,
Complaining loudly, 'Look at me!'
They wiggle and giggle on the ground,
Their wriggling charms are quite profound.

The sun laughs bright, the clouds wear smirks,
As garden gnomes tease shy little jerks.
With silly dances, they share the space,
Each little plant a smiling face.

A squirrel steals seeds like a crafty thief,
Dropping some nuts, causing some grief.
But in this chaos, there's joy, it seems,
Nature's laughter fills the beams.

Fragrance of Forgotten Times

Once I met a rose so red,
It claimed it painted the town instead.
While tulips giggled, bowed their heads,
"Stop boasting, dear; we all know you're bred!"

A daffodil stretched, reaching for fame,
While daisies whispered—'What a shame!'
But all in jest, they shared a jest,
Their laughter echoed, feeling blessed.

Old herbs reminisced about the past,
Swapping tales from shadows cast.
Each leaf contributed to the lore,
Sharing memories forever more.

In sunlit hours, their spirits grew,
As breezes danced and laughter flew.
In this fragrant, joyous heap,
Garden secrets they all keep.

Secret Garden Symphony

In a corner where wildflowers meet,
The sunflowers sway to a happy beat.
They nod and hum with quite a flair,
While butterflies dance, flipping through air.

The lilies gossip with cheeky laughs,
Reciting sonnets of playful gaffes.
"Did you see that bee fall flat?"
While snickering hard, they shared their chat.

In the shade, a spider spun a yarn,
Of tangled webs and dandelion charm.
With every twist, he drew a grin,
In this wild symphony, they all win.

The wind creaked jokes through leafy lines,
Tickling blooms with gentle signs.
Nature's orchestra, brightly done,
In the secret garden, pure fun!

Tales of the Blooming Hearts

In a meadow where laughter grows,
Each petal and leaf a tale bestows.
A shy lilac blushed as bees would buzz,
While neighboring roses waved—"What a fuzz!"

Fragrant stories through gardens drift,
Each whiff a memory, a silly gift.
The daisies plotted a raucous prank,
As honeybees just lolled in rank.

Snapdragons sparked tales of might,
With blooming banter, pure delight.
In the tales of those brave blooms,
Laughter unraveled in the rooms.

So here's to flowers, our cheerful friends,
With whimsical charms that never end.
In every garden, joy imparts,
The happiest tales of blooming hearts.

Dancing in the Sunlight

Beneath a sky so bright and clear,
The flowers twist, they sway, they cheer.
A bumblebee is on the run,
He trips right over—oh, what fun!

With petals out, they flutter fast,
A dance-off in the sunlight cast.
One little stem does the moonwalk,
While ladybugs in circles talk.

The leaves are laughing, what a sight,
A butterfly takes flight, so light.
The tulips giggle, 'You're so grand!'
While daisies try their best to stand.

And as the sun begins to rest,
They flop and drop, give it their best.
In twilight's glow, they take a bow,
Dancing dreams for tomorrow's vow.

Crimson Echoes

A flash of red, like glitzy shoes,
The petals shout, 'We've got the blues!'
They wave their arms, they stomp their feet,
In blooming boots, they feel the beat.

The sun comes in; they strike a pose,
And tickle bees right on the nose.
A squirrel stops to stare in glee,
'You flowers think you're funnier than me?'

A bud replies with such great flair,
'We're blooming legends, don't you dare!
Try dancing with us, show your stuff,
But watch your tail, it might get tough!'

So sunlight fades, they end the show,
With petals drooping nice and slow.
What echoes linger, full of cheer,
The funniest blooms, we hold so dear!

Heartstrings of Flora

A flower strums a leafy chord,
While others hum, they can't afford!
'Let's sing a song of bright delight,
While pesky ants march in a line.'

With every note, the stems all sway,
And little bugs jump in to play.
A ladybug, a tiny star,
Bears harmony, but sings off-bar!

The sun beams down, a spotlight bright,
As petals blush with pure delight.
They swing and shake, a floral band,
While wind provides a gentle hand.

Oh, what a show, the laughter roars,
When daisies play on grassy floors.
They pack it in as night descends,
With heartstrings strong, and laughter bends.

Source of the Sun

In gardens green, where laughter's spun,
The flowers claim they're number one.
With stems all tall, they strike a pose,
'We're the source, as everyone knows!'

The daisies snicker, 'Don't be so rude,
We sparkle bright, with cheeky food!'
A sunflower winks, 'I'm on the rise,
With towering dreams, oh what a surprise!'

As shadows stretch, they tell their tales,
Of clumsy bees and playful gales.
Each bloom a gem, of color and cheer,
They twirl together, year after year.

So when the sun dips low in the sky,
They bask in glory, and wink goodbye.
In every petal, there's laughter found,
The source of joy, in blooms around.

Colors of the Soul

In the garden, colors play,
A purple bird went on its way.
The daisies giggled in delight,
While sunflowers danced in the light.

A cat who thought she could sing,
Chased butterflies with a flap of wing.
The roses blushed, they knew they were fine,
As they whispered secrets of the vine.

A rainbow snickered from the sky,
As weeds plotted a scheme nearby.
With each shade, mishaps unfold,
Nature's humor, bright and bold.

Splendor in the Soil

Down in the dirt, things are alive,
Earthworms wiggled, making a jive.
Potatoes dream of being fries,
While radishes giggle with surprise.

In the mud, the critters play games,
Making up silly nicknames for flames.
The carrots whisper, 'We're pretty neat',
While onions cry over their own defeat.

Fungi fashion trendy hats,
As beetles wear mismatched spats.
With every squish underfoot in the mud,
Life in the soil is a funny flood!

Echoing Vibrance

In the meadow where daisies sway,
A squirrel threw a bright bouquet.
The daffodils laughed, 'What a show!'
As dandelions cheered, 'We're in the flow!'

A pesky bee buzzed, causing a stir,
As tulips shimmied, chasing the blur.
Sunlight sparkled, a disco ball,
While shadows twirled, they had a ball.

Laughter echoed through the breeze,
As flowers whispered, 'What's the tease?'
Nature's chorus, wild and spry,
In vibrant hues, they wave goodbye.

Nature's Painted Palette

A canvas waits to burst with cheer,
Each brushstroke brightens the atmosphere.
The trees wear coats of emerald green,
While flowers compete in a colorful scene.

A hedgehog rolled in yellow clay,
Thinking he could paint his own way.
Splashing colors, a joyful mess,
The artist nature sings 'Yes, yes!'

Clouds dripped hues, a playful stain,
Unruly shades fell like rain.
In this gallery, laughter shall reign,
Nature's whim blends joy and pain.

Glimmers of Growth

In the garden, things get loud,
Plants wear hats, the bugs feel proud.
A chorus blooms, the petals cheer,
Each tiny leaf whispers, 'We're here!'

Sunshine giggles, the rain gives a wink,
Roots plot a dance over the brink.
A daisy shimmies, a stem takes a bow,
While the weeds mutter, 'O, not now!'

Frogs join the band, croak out a tune,
As butterflies flutter, swooping in June.
The soil's party has just begun,
Each little sprout is having its fun!

So raise a pot, offer some cheer,
In the realm of green, there's nothing to fear.
With laughter in leaves, the world comes alive,
In this garden, oh how we thrive!

Moonlit Blossoms

Under the stars, the petals play,
With moonbeams dancing, they sway away.
A tulip shouts, 'Come join the fun!'
While daisies giggle, 'We're second to none!'

Moths in tuxedos flit about,
While crickets sing, oh, without a doubt.
The night sky drips with sprightly charm,
Nature's antics, nothing can harm!

The jasmine winks, the night is young,
With herbal whispers, the night is sung.
Lavender pranks, spritzing with glee,
In moonlit mischief, we're wild and free!

So raise your stems and let laughter bloom,
In nighttime's embrace, there's endless room.
We'll dance till dawn, with colors so bright,
A party of petals, the ultimate night!

The Colorful Conclave

Colors convene, they gather around,
Each petal dressed, as legends abound.
The reds tell tales of passionate flings,
While whites ponder deep philosophical things.

Rugged bluebells boast their wide stance,
As every green leaf joins in the dance.
Yellow laughs, says, 'I'm full of light!'
They plot for the day, oh what a sight!

Orange quips, 'I'm zestier, you see!'
While violets pipe in, 'We're royalty!'
They chuckle and chortle, a vivid parade,
In this colorful hustle, they're never afraid.

As petals collide in this joyful jest,
Nature's debate puts laughter to the test.
In leafy conclaves, with humor it seems,
The world is brightened with floral dreams!

Between the Sunshine

Among the rays, a bumblebee hums,
As petals pop, and the shy flower drums.
A daisy declares, 'Let's throw a bash!'
While sunflowers giggle, their faces all splash.

In the midst of warmth, a laughter erupts,
As critters gather, nature's hiccup.
The herbs join in with their spicy flair,
Chasing the clouds, a comedic affair!

A poppy starts spinning, twirling around,
With tulips laughing at such a sound.
'Who knew we could groove on the grass?' they say,
In joyous abandon, they brighten the day!

So come join the fun, let your worries fly,
In the blooms of sunlight, let laughter amplify.
For in every petal, there's glee to be found,
In the garden of mirth, where joy knows no bound!

Velvet Flora Under a Starlit Sky

In the garden of whispers, plants take a dance,
Their leaves in suspense, twirling at chance.
A flower wears velvet, with polka dots bright,
Sipping on moonbeams while blocking the light.

Bumblebees buzzing, in tuxedos so grand,
They've planned a gala, all pollen at hand.
The petals are giggling, with secrets to share,
In a soirée of scents, do we scents bother? Nah!

The crickets play music from deep in the grass,
While roses play drums made of old window glass.
They tap to the rhythm of the night's gentle sway,
As the tulips drink lemonade, shouting, "Hey!"

Underneath stars, a cat joins the fun,
Sipping on dew drops, while basking in sun.
The velvet flora sparkles, as laughter erupts,
In this leafy cabaret, where whimsy erupts.

A Palette of Passionate Petals

A painter came strolling, with brushes in tow,
He spotted some blossoms all painted in glow.
With colors so vivid, they struck up a pose,
Said, "Please, don't go wild, stick to basics, who knows?"

The daisies declared, "Let's daub with a splash,
We're bold, we're unique, and we love a good clash!"
So they painted their petals in stripes and in dots,
Confusing the bees, they forgot all the plots.

A sunflower laughed, claimed he needed a crown,
While the violets giggled, and threatened to frown.
The tulips all chimed in with a flamboyant air,
"Let's make this a party, with flair beyond compare!"

But the paint ran away, as the rain started pouring,
And flowers were left, with no colors restoring.
Yet they swayed in the breeze, their funny parade,
In a palette of petals where laughter just played.

Chasing the Palette of Dawn

In the light of the morn, as the sun starts to peek,
The flowers start plotting, they're loud, not discreet.
"Let's dye our morning heads in orange and pink,
And prank all the bees, make them stop and rethink!"

The lilies say, "Watch, we'll call in the ducks,
We'll teach them to dance, then we'll steal their 'quacks'!"
While the pansies were staging a comical play,
They made all the petals shout hip-hip-hooray!

"Who needs morning coffee, when petals can perk?
Let's tickle the tulips, make those bedheads lurk!"
As the colors burst forth in silly display,
The dawn couldn't help but just laugh in its way.

So the flowers kept giggling, as morning unfurled,
Creating a ruckus, painting bright the world.
Chasing the light, they spun round and round,
In a whimsical dance, where joy could be found.

The Heartbeat of a Flower

Underneath the petals, a secret does beat,
With each little thrum, it dances, so sweet.
The hibiscus wears sneakers, ready to play,
While the daisies do pushups—it's quite the display!

They link up in circles, skipping and hopping,
The blossoms unite, no sign of them stopping.
"Oh, feel that heart thump? It's music to bloom,
A rhythm of laughter that's lighting the room!"

A tulip then shouted, "Let's throw a bouquet,
With confetti of laughter, we'll brighten the day!"
Though the roses got tangled, tangled in fun,
They spun in their petals, as bright as the sun.

So if you see flowers, with giggles and cheer,
Know their heartbeat sings, make it crystal clear.
In gardens of humor, where color is loud,
Be life among petals; just dance, be proud!

Luminescence of Nature

In the garden, colors burst,
A pink that dances, never cursed.
The bees are buzzing, oh what glee,
They bump and crash, just wait and see.

Petals giggle in the sun,
A floral dance, oh what fun!
The dew drops play, they slide and glide,
Each flower grins, full of pride.

A bumblebee slips, a comical sight,
Spinning round in pure delight.
With every bloom, their antics soar,
Nature's jester, forevermore.

So come and join, this botanic show,
Where laughter blooms and colors flow.
A patchwork quilt of joy and cheer,
In this garden, life is dear.

Palette of Paradise

Find the shades of silly dreams,
In petals soft as whipped-up creams.
Orange and yellow, a fruity mess,
Nature's palette, we must confess.

Blue shoes on daisies, how absurd!
Silly thoughts, they spin and whirled.
Marigolds wearing hats of green,
A floral fashion show, quite the scene.

Each stem a joke, each leaf a pun,
With every glance, we burst with fun.
The poppies wink, the violets tease,
A riot of colors that aim to please.

So grab a brush, and paint it right,
With laughter spilling, day and night.
In this garden, let's all partake,
A joyful canvas, make no mistake.

The Attire of Dawn

Morning mist wears a floral show,
Lilies shrug as breezes blow.
A sunflower dons a flashy gown,
While daisies spin, twirling round.

The sun peeks up, a laughing face,
Wearing hues of bright embrace.
A wardrobe change, oh what a fuss,
Nature's runway, join the trust.

Tulips prance in rainbow styles,
Their fashion sense, they flaunt with smiles.
Frogs in bow ties, a sight to see,
Nature's party, you and me.

So let's applaud this dawn's parade,
With every flower, a joke is made.
In petals' laughter, bright and clear,
The day begins, come join the cheer!

Floral Adventures Await

To the garden, off we dash,
Where petals play and colors clash.
Roses ride on a grape-soda breeze,
Pansies prank, with giggles that tease.

Oh look, a daffodil in a cap!
Taking a nap on a fluffy lap.
Petals splash in a puddle of dew,
Chasing butterflies, just us two.

Hiccups of laughter fill the air,
As daisies tumble without a care.
Nature's game, a hidden quest,
With every flower, we're truly blessed.

So join the fun, don't hesitate,
These floral friends can't wait to mate.
In this land of bloom and play,
Adventure calls, hip-hip-hooray!

Celestial Blooms

In a garden of dreams where colors dance,
Flowers wear smiles, in a joyful prance.
With petals so bright, they giggle and sway,
Tickling the sun in a playful display.

Grasshoppers leap like they own the place,
While bees throw a party, all about space.
A daffodil winks with a cheeky twist,
As daisies conspire, 'Don't let them assist!'

Sunshine joins in with a burst of glee,
Painting the flowers in a vibrant spree.
The wind joins the fun, swirling around,
A symphony of laughter, crisp sounds abound.

At dusk when the stars twinkle above,
The blooms share secrets, giggling with love.
They tuck in their petals for the night's nap,
In the universe of flowers, none find a gap.

The Harmony of Color

A tangle of shades in a foray bright,
Petals plot mischief deep into the night.
Roses chuckle, "That hue's such a cheat!"
While violets argue who's more sweet.

The yellows complain of being too loud,
While the greens insist they're the most proud.
A painted lady lands, stirs up a fuss,
"What's this hullabaloo? It's simply a plus!"

In this playful squabble of pigment and cheer,
The flowers unite, saying, "Let's persevere!"
Underneath the moon, they share a good joke,
With giggles and snickers, the petals bespoke.

Though colors may clash in a raucous ballet,
Deep down, they know they can share the day.
Together they bloom, in their colorful spree,
Creating a canvas of sheer harmony.

Adventures in the Garden

Beneath the sun where mischief springs,
A gnome's gone missing, oh what tomfoolery brings!
With pots on their heads, the turtles embark,
On quests for the weeds that steal the park.

A munching caterpillar shares a wild tale,
Of a runaway snail setting up a sail.
"Did you see the daffodils, all in a spin?"
"Or the roses rolling over, who let them in?"

The daisies decided to host a fair,
With pancakes for pollen, who wouldn't dare?
Bumblebees swing with a jazzier flair,
While ants bring the snacks, working without a care.

As night sweeps in, escapades unfold,
With fireflies shining, their laughter bold.
Tomorrow brings more, with the dawn's early light,
In this garden of laughter, everything feels right.

Sunkissed Delights

Sun-kissed petals play peek-a-boo,
Winks from the daisies, playful and true.
Butterflies flutter in a whimsical race,
"Catch us if you can!" they tease with a face.

The marigolds boast, "We're the life of the party!"
While sunflowers grin, "We're just getting hearty!"
A squash plant giggles, "I'll sprout with flair!"
But a bean stalk shouts, "Hey, don't forget air!"

With laughter a-bloom, the day slips away,
As shadows lengthen and colors sway.
The night blooms a chorus, of sounds pure and bright,
In this garden of joy, all hearts feel light.

So raise up your cups, let's toast to the shine,
Where fun finds a way to twist the divine.
In petals of glory, we'll dance and delight,
In a world so whimsical, under the night.

Botanical Ballads

In my garden, quite a sight,
Flowers dance in morning light.
A bee buzzes, claims its space,
While worms wiggle, join the race.

Petals bright, a silly scene,
Sunflowers grinning, green beans lean.
Lettuce laughing in the breeze,
Oh what fun among the leaves!

Beets wear hats, their tops so high,
Carrots giggle as they sigh.
Nature's jokes scattered around,
With each bloom, new laughs abound.

Visions in Bloom

There's a daisy with a grin,
Sighting all the flies within.
Gifts from nature, sweet delight,
Roses blushing with their might.

Tulips do the honky-tonk,
While violets love to prank and bonk.
Nature's laughter fills the air,
A floral fest beyond compare!

Cacti wearing stylish hats,
Making friends with all the rats.
Petals twirling, oh so grand,
Dancing wildly in the sand.

The Essence of Nature's Palette

In the patch, colors clash,
Tulips giggle, daffodils dash.
Marigolds in orange attire,
Caught in a hilarious quagmire.

Sunflowers stretching towards the sky,
Hoping birds won't pass them by.
With leafy friends all in line,
Making jokes that bloom like wine.

Pansies wear the brightest frowns,
While peas plan their little towns.
Nature's spark, a playful spree,
Joyful plants, come laugh with me!

Ecstasy in Each Petal

Petals whisper secrets sweet,
While daisies tap their little feet.
Butterflies doing pirouettes,
Celebrating smaller bets.

Lavender prancing, looking fly,
Chasing shadows as they cry.
Buds bursting with cheeky charms,
Waving wildly with soft arms.

Ferns discussing wild intrigues,
Giggling softly, oh the leagues!
Nature's humor, plain to see,
Join the fun, come bloom with me!

Tales from the Flower Patch

In the garden, plants unite,
With hats and ties, they share delight.
A sunflower winks with a cheeky grin,
Says, "Join the fiesta, let the fun begin!"

Roses gossip 'neath leafy shade,
While daisies dance in the sun's parade.
The violets chuckle, oh what a sight,
As peonies tell tales of love at first light.

Carrots wear socks, quite out of place,
While radishes roll in a leafy race.
Lettuce laughs, "You should see my hair!"
The whole patch echoes with giggles in air.

In this patch, such quirks abound,
Every blossom is joyfully crowned.
So, come my friend, take a stroll and see,
Where flowers and laughter grow wild and free.

Whispers of Nature

The tulips tell secrets in vibrant hues,
"We party all night, without any snooze!"
Daffodils chuckle at passing bees,
"Our nectar's prime; come, sip if you please!"

Buttercups giggle at clouds up above,
"Are they pillows sent down, or just fluffs of love?"
They sway with the breeze in happy delight,
While bumblebees zip in a candy-like flight.

Petunias pout when raindrops fall,
"Quit your crying, it's just nature's call!"
With every sprinkle, a joyous new game,
They burst into laughter, and tease the same.

If you listen close, you'll hear their song,
The whispers of nature where all things belong.
In this silly symphony, every bloom shines,
Merriment woven through the tendrils of vines.

Petals and Possibilities

Dancing petals float in mid-air,
Wiggly worms join without a care.
"Why so serious?" a snapdragon calls,
"Let's unleash giggles within these walls!"

With bees wearing glasses, quite the charade,
They argue over which flower's the grade.
"Look here!" cries a daisy, "I'm quite the sight!"
While tulips wink, grinning with all their might.

The daisies decree it's a uniform day,
Everybody's dressed in their floral ballet.
Even the weeds wear their sass with pride,
In this rambunctious garden, joy can't hide!

Join the frolic, where laughter is free,
In a whirlwind of petals, just come see!
Where every bloom tells a tale truly bright,
And every laugh chases away the night.

The Abode of Blossoms

Welcome, my friend, to a bloom-filled home,
Where flowers gossip and giggle and roam.
The sunflowers toast in their tall, golden hats,
Swapping tales of rabbits and playful sprats.

Pink roses complain, "It's so hot today!"
While violets chill in their cool, shady bay.
Petals are fluttering, creating a show,
As the bumblebees dance with a wild, silly flow.

Geraniums chuckle, "We missed all the fun!"
As marigolds burst into bloom with the sun.
"It's all in good times, you know it's true,
In the abode of blossoms, there's always room for you!"

With puns, smiles, and even a wink,
Nature's comedy will make you rethink.
So traipse through the petals, don't be shy,
In this floral abode, the laughter won't die!

Blooms Bound by Time

In the garden, petals dance,
Winking at bees, they take a chance.
Time tricks the blooms, they feel so spry,
But wait—are those roots tangled up, oh my?

Sunshine hugs them, morning bright,
Yet they plot mischief all through the night.
With whispers of wind, they get quite bold,
Forgetting they're flowers, not legends of old.

So they prank each other, giggle and sway,
Switching their scents like a playful ballet.
One blooms pink, the other goes blue,
Confusing the gardeners, what a hullabaloo!

But come the frost, they huddle tight,
Sharing their tales, of summer's delight.
In every petal, a chuckle remains,
Bound by the memories, a bouquet of stains.

Floral Fantasies

Peeking through leaves, a bright pot glows,
A cluster of colors, as everybody knows.
Each bloom has a secret, a dream up its sleeve,
A fantasy garden, just waiting to weave.

One petal declares it's an airplane to fly,
While another insists it's an ice cream pie.
They giggle and chatter, the colors collide,
As they spin silly stories, unable to hide.

In this patch of laughter where laughter resides,
The green leaves are jesters, where whimsy abides.
Trying new outfits, they dress bold and sassy,
In polka dots petals, they look oh so classy!

As evening approaches, they share their dreams,
Of wild, silly antics and fanciful schemes.
Each bloom drifts to sleep, with a chuckle and sigh,
In their floral fantasy, they soar to the sky.

Revelations in Reddish Hues

Oh red little blossoms, with tales to impart,
Whispers abound, you play the part.
With each gentle sway, you spill your thoughts,
Confessing your secrets, in jangly knots.

One reveled how once it glittered in sun,
But secretly longed to outrun everyone.
While another planned a mischievous race,
To see who could tickle the gardener's face.

They brag about fragrance, stealing the show,
With scents so sweet, they steal hearts in row.
Yet late in the twilight, they swap funny woes,
As each petal laughs, through laughter it grows.

So here in the garden, the red blooms unite,
Sharing their stories, both silly and bright.
With a wink and a laugh, in the warm evening dew,
These revelations glimmer in reddish hue.

Shades of Happiness

In a pot, they dance with glee,
Waving petals, wild and free.
Bright as candy, bold and loud,
They giggle, drawing quite a crowd.

With every splash of vibrant hue,
They whisper secrets, funny too.
Tickled by the morning sun,
A jaunty jig, they have such fun.

Buzzy bees join in the spree,
Dancing round so merrily.
A bumble in a flowery hat,
Sipping nectar, how about that?

As blooms compete for silly laughs,
Each petal forms its own kind of paths.
In this garden, joys expand,
A colorful world at our command.

Vibrant Murmurs

Listen close, they tell a tale,
Of cheeky ants that tip the scale.
With every rustle, giggles soar,
A leafy laugh, who could ask for more?

Spinning twirls in sunny rays,
They swap their socks on silly days.
The violets roll their eyes with flair,
While daisies breathe the fragrant air.

A ladybug with polka spots,
Joined the fray in two small knots.
Together, they create a scene,
Of whispered laughter, bright and green.

Soon the garden holds its breath,
For fun and games, they dance with zest.
Small wonders twinkle in the light,
As petals cheer in sheer delight.

The Colorful Chronicles

Once upon a burst of bloom,
A tulip wore a silly plume.
With giggles sprouting from each stem,
A frolicsome, flowery diadem.

The cosmos cracked a joke or two,
While pansies rolled their eyes at view.
Bouncing petals, here and there,
Unfurling stories, without a care.

Each color splashes here and there,
Like puns that dance upon the air.
A riot of shades, a joyous feast,
In this happy garden, joy won't cease.

With sunshine and a friendly breeze,
The blooms conspire to tease and please.
Oh, how delightfully they bloom,
Creating laughter, room by room.

Blooms Beneath the Stars

When twilight falls on petal bright,
The blooms all gather for a light.
With moonbeams glimmering on their hats,
They swap their stories, raising chats.

Daisies dream of twinkling ships,
While tulips practice their funny quips.
The fragrant air, a stage for jest,
Each bloom competing for the best.

Starry nights ignite the scene,
Where colors mingle, bright and keen.
Each petal sparkles, winks a bit,
In this floral comedy skit.

As laughter rises all around,
A merry harmony is found.
With giggles echoing, bright and bold,
These cheerful blooms, a joy to behold.

Seasons of Passion

In spring, they dance with cheer,
Little petals, bright and dear.
They flirt and sway, a playful sight,
Whispering jokes 'til late at night.

Summer sun, a hot affair,
Colors burst, with joy to share.
They giggle in the warmth and glow,
Telling secrets only they know.

Autumn comes, they start to tease,
Flaunting reds with gentle ease.
Winds of change, they swirl around,
Hiding laughter in the ground.

Winter's chill, a freeze-frame fun,
Sparkling frosts as bright as sun.
They shiver but they laugh, oh so,
Counting flakes, a funny show.

Petal Poetry

In each bloom, a tale unfolds,
Words of laughter, whispers bold.
Petals sketched with silly quips,
Tickling hearts with funny slips.

In the garden, jokes abound,
Nature's giggles all around.
Listening closely, you'll hear the puns,
Laughter sprouting in the sun.

Even bees join in the jest,
Buzzing by to be their guest.
Spreading joy from bloom to bloom,
Creating smiles that chase the gloom.

So come along, don't be shy,
Join the petals, let laughter fly.
In every flower, a cheerful tongue,
In petal poetry, joy is sung.

The Heart's Garden

In the garden where hearts meet,
Petals play at nature's feet.
With every color, a new surprise,
Tickling fancies and brightening skies.

The sunflowers wink a cheerful grin,
While daisies blush from deep within.
With each bloom, a playful tease,
Crafting giggles with the breeze.

Roses plot with petals rare,
Whispering jokes to stop despair.
In this garden of silly schemes,
Laughter flows like sweet sunbeams.

So venture forth, and don't delay,
Join the frolic, let's laugh and sway.
In the heart's garden, joy's the aim,
And all the flowers play the game.

In Each Bloom's Embrace

In each bloom, a wink and smile,
Playing tricks that last a while.
Colors bright as laughter's tune,
Joking gently with the moon.

Lilies laugh in whispered tones,
Sharing laughter with the stones.
In their embrace, a giggle grows,
A funny secret that nobody knows.

With every bud, a jest unfolds,
Nature's art, the heart beholds.
So bloom with joy, let spirits lift,
In the garden, life's a gift.

And as we stroll through fragrant air,
Join the blooms, shed every care.
In each petal's playful grace,
Discover joy in every space.

Kaleidoscope of Color

In a pot with whimsy, they dance,
Petals wearing polka dots, with chance.
Each one a quirky tale to share,
As bees buzz by without a care.

Sunshine laughs, the soil winks,
They chat in colors, bright links.
A purple blush, a crimson sigh,
Who knew plants had such a high?

When rain comes down, they wear a frown,
Muddy feet in nature's gown.
But with the sun, they'll cheer once more,
Turning gardens into folklore!

So grab a chair, pull up a seat,
Join the blooms, enjoy the beat.
In this riot of shades, we find,
A chuckle shared, our hearts entwined.

The Blooming Chronicles

There once was a flower named Phil,
With petals he'd stretch, what a thrill!
He dreamed of fame, bright lights galore,
"Give me a role!" he cried, "I want more!"

His buddy, a bud named Claire,
Said, "Grow up, dear, do take care!
Fame's just pollen—light and sweet,
But oh, the roots can't take the heat!"

They plotted a show, a grand debut,
With worms as guests and bees in queue.
But when they danced, they tripped and fell,
Creating a scene, oh what a spell!

Yet giggles rang from the leafy crowd,
For every tumble, they cheered aloud.
No matter the bloom, or how they sway,
In the garden of laughs, they stole the day.

Nature's Vibrant Tapestry

In a world where greens collide,
A silly flower rode a tide.
With stripes of orange and dots of blue,
It danced away, oh what a view!

A sunflower tried to steal the show,
Complaining loudly, "Hey, let me glow!"
But the tiny blooms, all round and spry,
Challenged the big, to reach for the sky.

They had a race and spun around,
Petals flying, colors unbound.
The butterflies giggled, as they flew by,
Watching this spectacle with a sly eye.

And so they played till the day was done,
Creating a riot—a blooming fun.
In this tapestry, wild and bright,
Nature's laughter echoes in the night.

The Language of Leaves

In whispers soft, the leaves confide,
"Why do flowers wear their pride?"
They giggle and sway, in a leafy jest,
While buds in bloom puff out their chest.

"I see your color, that shade of green,
But look at this petal—oh so keen!"
The leaves shoot back, with a rustling cheer,
"Your bloom may fade, but I'm always here!"

A vine creeps close, with a twist and turn,
"Let's join the fun, it's our turn to churn!"
With a flip and a flop, they start to sway,
Becoming the life of a leafy ballet.

So when you wander through nature's way,
Listen closely, the plants have their say.
In this garden of chuckles and leafy dreams,
Even the ordinary bursts at the seams!

Fragrance of Forgotten Dreams

In the garden where scents collide,
The daisies gossip, the tulips chide.
A daffodil trips, loud laughter ensues,
As sunbeams dance in playful hues.

Petals whisper secrets of days gone past,
Each bloom a tale, too silly to last.
With bees in bow ties and ants in gowns,
They've turned this patch into laughter towns.

A rose with a quip, a violet with flair,
Who knew flowers could have such a care?
They brew sunlit jokes over morning tea,
Giggling softly, just you and me.

So let's plant joy, let's sow the fun,
With each little sprout, a chuckle begun.
In this fragrant land of whimsical beams,
We'll wander forever in forgotten dreams.

Jewel-Toned Epiphanies

In a patch of color, the petals unite,
Emerald leaves make the laughter ignite.
A sapphire bloom with a wink in its eye,
Cracks a wise joke as the butterflies fly.

Sunshine's a thief in this radiant scene,
Stealing the warmth, leaving giggles unseen.
With rubies and topaz in frolicsome throng,
Each flower is singing its own silly song.

The marigolds prance in their gold and bright cheer,
While pansies roll out their comedic frontier.
With laughter afloat in the breeze, oh so clear,
Even the weeds join in raucous career!

So gather the blooms in a bouquet of joy,
In colors that twinkle, in laughter, oh boy!
For each hue holds a giggle, a chuckle, a glee,
In jewel-toned laughter, come dance with me!

Threads of Earthly Beauty

Embroidered petals, a tapestry spun,
Of giggles and winks as the day's just begun.
A sunflower chuckles, its seeds take a flight,
While daisies wear crowns in the morning light.

The violets knit stories of fanciful fun,
Where bumblebees zoom and the laughter's a run.
Every bloom has a quirk, a whimsical tale,
In this tapestry bright, we shall never grow pale.

Tangled in humor, the blossoms conspire,
With laughter as thick as a well-planned attire.
Each petal a thread in the fabric of cheer,
Weaving joy into hearts that we hold so dear.

So let's sow the seeds, let's craft our delight,
In this wonderful garden, all sunny and bright.
With threads of mischief and colors so bold,
We'll share in the laughter, and never grow old!

Echoes in the Floral Cosmos

In the cosmos of blooms where petals convene,
Echoes of laughter can often be seen.
A daisy throws back its head and it giggles,
While a shy little lilac just jumps in and wiggles.

Comets of colors shoot across the sky,
With coreopsis shining like stars up high.
A group of bold tulips play hide-and-seek,
In this floral expanse, no quiet, no meek!

Chasing the scents like a playful parade,
The flowers arrange their own comical charade.
With each rustle of leaves, a joke finds its way,
In the echo of laughter, let's frolic and play!

So we'll dance with the blooms under cosmos so wide,
With petals and smiles as our laughter's guide.
In the echoes of joy, we'll forever abide,
In this floral adventure, let merriment ride!

Whispers of the Bloom

In a garden, quite absurd,
Flowers gossip, oh how they've stirred!
Petals giggle, leaves make a fuss,
Roses blush, it's all so bused.

Buzzing bees with tiny hats,
Dancing 'round like acrobats.
A daisy wearing thick-set specs,
Claims it's the smartest of flower sects!

Sunbeams tickle, shadows play,
Violets shout, 'It's a sunny day!'
Tulips dance to a silent tune,
Wiggling under the watching moon.

In this patch of sheer delight,
Bugs make jokes, quite a sight!
With each bloom, a tale will bloom,
In the garden, there's no gloom.

The Scarlet Serenade

Oh, the reds and pinks parade,
With each petal, a new charade!
Hummingbirds with bowties neat,
    Join the flowers for a treat.

Tulips trumpet with great flair,
As daisies do a moonlit air.
A sign reads, 'Welcome all to dance!'
    Even weeds join in the prance!

Green grubs sport their shiniest caps,
    Teasing plants with little jabs.
As laughter echoes through the air,
A blossom winks, but none would care.

Now clovers roll in glee and laughter,
    Turning frowns to fun thereafter.
With every sway and petal's rise,
This bloom-cheer catches every eye.

Emerald Secrets

In the shade, oh what a scene,
Grasshoppers chatting, feeling keen.
A secret, hidden, deep beneath,
Where mint leaves sip on peppermint breath.

Lettuce wears its leafy crown,
While rhubarb dons a silly frown.
'What's the rumor?' the mints inquire,
As wildflowers jump, aiming higher!

Fuchsia blooms like it's on stage,
Telling stories of the garden's age.
With each rustle of hidden charms,
They create giggles and soft alarms.

In emerald shades, they plot and play,
Mixing mischief in their sway.
Through the laughter, the petals gleam,
As whispers float, chasing a dream.

Florets of Joy

Tiny florets with witty flair,
Waving like they don't have a care!
Chasing butterflies in a race,
Tickling each other, just face to face.

Petunias grinning with silly glee,
Dancing with a bee or three.
Sunflowers nodding, quite aware,
Of the gags pulled in the air!

Pansies laughing as clouds roll by,
Making fun of the big blue sky.
With each breeze, a pop of cheer,
Their whimsical ways draw everyone near.

In the bloom of joyous lore,
They reminisce and seek for more.
In this patch of color bright,
Nature's comedy is pure delight!

Vinyl Rustle of the Summer Wind

A petal floats down, it tickles my nose,
I sneeze and I cough, oh do I, goodness knows!
The sun's quite a joker, it plays peek-a-boo,
With flowers in hats, they're dancing for you!

Bees buzz by, wearing tiny black hats,
They gossip and joke like chattering cats.
A butterfly flutters, it thinks it's a star,
But trips on a leaf, oh, how funny you are!

The breeze carries laughter, and whispers, and cheer,
As plants play charades, "Guess what we are here!"
Their petals are giggling, it's such a delight,
Spring's silly blooms are a comical sight!

But watch out for ants, they march in a line,
They're plotting a dance, oh it's quite divine!
With pollen as confetti, they join in the fun,
A garden soirée has just begun!

Luminescence of Petal Dreams

In the garden of laughter, the colors collide,
A blue flower whispers to pink, "Let's hide!"
They play tag with shadows, jump over the sun,
A bouquet of giggles; oh, isn't this fun?

The daisies wear sunglasses, feeling quite cool,
While tulips are dancing, "We rule this old school!"
A bumblebee busts out the moves with a twist,
This flower fiesta is too grand to miss!

Pink blooms start cracking their jokes with a flair,
Each punchline blossoms in the warm summer air.
The daisies and lilies have never felt free,
In a waltz of the wild, oh, look at them spree!

Underneath the moonlight, a night show begins,
The flora's still laughing, as the party spins.
With petals a-glow in the soft silver beams,
This garden of wonders sparks petal dreams!

Floral Whispers of the Earth

"Hey look," says the bud with a wink and a jig,
"I can do a split, or just flop like a pig!"
The violets together do rolls in the dirt,
These frolicking flowers won't ever get hurt!

Dandelion wishes float out like balloons,
They giggle and shimmer like sunbeams at noon.
"Catch me if you can!" shouts the playful green leaf,
While it dodges the snorts from a gopher in grief.

Caterpillars munch on the vibes of the show,
"Do you think we can dance?" "Oh, let's give it a go!"
With wiggling bodies, they promise to twirl,
The concert of soil sends laughter to swirl!

In this garden stage, there's never a night,
When petals stop blooming and take off their light.
With tones of amusement, the flora sings free,
In sweet floral whispers that tickle you and me!

A Tapestry of Radiant Colors

A quilt of hues sprawls beneath the bright skies,
Each section of laughter, a sweet little prize.
The marigolds gloat in their bold orange flair,
While pansies crack up, like life's a fair affair!

With fuchsia balloons, the blooms start to sway,
They giggle and wiggle throughout the bright day.
"Oh, can you believe how we shimmer and shine?"
A rose turns and nods, "Yeah, darling, we're fine!"

Chrysanthemums chatter, a delightful old crew,
They share all their tales with a sprinkle of dew.
The cosmos snickers at the tulip's old hat,
"Oh dear, why's your style just as flat as a mat?"

The rainbow unfolds as petals unite,
With laughter and color, everything's right.
In this tapestry woven with mirth and with cheer,
The garden erupts in a comedic frontier!

In the Shadow of Verdant Dreams

In the garden where plants play,
Colors dance in bright array.
A squirrel steals a flower pot,
While the neighbors laugh a lot.

Bees buzz like they own the place,
Chasing petals, what a race!
A rabbit thinks he's Camouflage,
In the greens, he looks like a mirage.

The sun spills gold on leafy beds,
Worms are doing their acrobats.
Each flower's got a silly face,
In this wild and wacky space.

The gardener whispers with a grin,
'Who knew weeds could wear a pin?'
With every bloom, a story brings,
Of plants that dance and funny things.

The Gardener's Hidden Treasures

Beneath the soil, secrets hide,
Among the roots where critters bide.
A shovel's strike, a toad jumps high,
Thinking, 'Why did I even try?'

All the bulbs wear hats so bright,
Playing dress-up day and night.
In rows they stand, a fashion show,
Who knew they'd steal the garden glow?

Caterpillars have a feast,
While snail races are a beast.
Each plant laughs at the sun's warm rays,
In this realm of plant-filled pranks and plays.

But when the gardener walks on through,
The flowers giggle, 'Oh, how do!'
For every petal holds a jest,
In the soil's grand comedy fest.

Blossoms that Sing

Petals lift their voices bright,
In a chorus of delight.
Bees join in with buzzing tunes,
While crickets chirp beneath the moons.

Tulips sway, the daisies spin,
They giggle softly, 'Where to begin?'
With every note, a laugh erupts,
In the green, joy just corrupts.

Butterflies twirl with flair and grace,
Spreading laughter in this space.
Their colors twinkle, oh so loud,
Creating tunes that call the crowd.

Each flower blooms a funny rhyme,
Spicing up the happy time.
A garden filled with musical glee,
Where nature's teachers sing with glee!

Gardens of Enchantment and Grace

In the heart of blooms so fine,
Roses sip on summer wine.
Laughter ripples through the air,
As daisies play a game of dare.

Sunflowers wear the silliest frown,
Declaring they're the best in town.
Potatoes dance a jig in beds,
While mushrooms nod their little heads.

The hammock swings in leafy shade,
As butterflies plot their grand parade.
A garden gnome starts to sway,
Breaking into dance, hooray!

Yet when the night begins to fall,
The stars join in with a glowing call.
In this patch, where nonsense thrives,
Laughter keeps the magic alive.

Colors of Continuity

In a pot of green and red,
A plant dreams of its bread.
With petals like socks unpaired,
It giggles, saying, "Who's scared?"

Dancing in the morning sun,
Waving at the bees for fun.
It sprinkles joy on the ground,
In a world so colorful, profound.

Shimmers of Flora

There's a bloom that likes to tease,
Tickling the air with a wheeze.
With leaves that wiggle and squirm,
It plots to take over the worm!

A close-up shot reveals the fun,
Sparkling like a shiny bun.
Blowing kisses to the breeze,
It plays games with naughty bees.

Enigma of the Blossoms

What's this flower trying to say?
Whispering secrets in a play.
Its petals spin tales untold,
Of socks lost in a laundry fold!

It mixes colors like a fool,
In hues that make us all drool.
As it winks and waves its hand,
Inviting all to its grandstand.

A Garden's Heartbeat

Booming laughter from the ground,
Where silly sprouts are often found.
Each stem sways to its own beat,
Plant-dancing with two left feet!

A gardener's crown, it claims with pride,
As gnomes in the corners abide.
In nature's circus, it plays a role,
A lightened heart, a joyful soul.

Nature's Crown of Rich Splendor

In leafy realms where blossoms laugh,
A crown of colors, nature's craft.
Bees wear tuxedos, buzzing so loud,
Dancing like kings before a proud crowd.

Petals shake hands with fluttering bees,
Tickling the air with fragrant trees.
Sunbeams play hopscotch on dew-dropped leaves,
Whispering secrets, oh how it weaves!

A rabbit in shades, with shades on its eyes,
Claims it's the coolest, so full of surprise.
While squirrels hold court on the tallest branch,
Debating the merits of a nutty dance!

Nature's a jester, with blooms like a jest,
Spreading pure joy, a vibrant fest.
In this garden, everyone's a clown,
Wearing a smile, the crown of renown.

Scarlet Sighs in the Morning Light.

Morning spills laughter with hues of bright red,
A chorus of petals prepare for their bed.
With yawns and a stretch, the roses awake,
Tickled by sunlight, their slumber they shake.

Bumblebees dance in a wobbly line,
Attempting a tango, they call it divine.
While daisies giggle and share their sweet lore,
Complaining about bees that swarm by the score.

A ladybug whispers, 'Life's quite absurd,'
As a butterfly tumbles and nearly gets stirred.
They gather for gossip, all dressed in their best,
In this vivid world, humor's never at rest.

With every new dawn, a show is displayed,
In floral hijinks, all worries allayed.
Scarlet sighs echo, no hint of despair,
In petals and laughter, they float through the air.

Petals of Resilience

Amidst the garden, laughter springs forth,
Petals stand tall, showcasing their worth.
A daisy, half-hearted, claims it's a star,
While marigolds giggle from near and afar.

Wind chimes their secrets in breezy delight,
As flowers exchange tales of scaling new heights.
'You wilting already?' the daisies would tease,
While a tulip rolls back, trying to sneeze!

A cactus with style dons a hat from the whims,
And declares it's the sharpest of all garden hymns.
While squirrels debate if nuts should be sown,
In a quest for the treasure they've somehow outgrown.

Each petal a story, of courage and fun,
With laughter and color, they bask in the sun.
In gardens of whimsy, there's no room for gloom,
Petals of resilience always make room!

Secrets in Scarlet

Beneath the red blooms, such mischief they keep,
Whispers and giggles beneath twilight's leap.
Roses confide in the mischievous breeze,
Trading their tales with the buzzing of bees.

A group of tulips plots a bright escapade,
While violets chuckle, checking their parade.
The poppies propose a grand flower show,
Where mischief's the prize, and laughter will flow.

A snail dons a cape, declares it's a queen,
Ruling the patch where all antics convene.
With petals a-twirl and laughter in tow,
They plan silly stunts, as gardens bestow.

In twilight's embrace, their secrets unfold,
In hues of scarlet, their stories are told.
Where fun is the key, and friendship the gem,
In this blooming world, they're all just ahem!

www.ingramcontent.com/pod-product-compliance
Ingram Content Group UK Ltd.
Pitfield, Milton Keynes, MK11 3LW, UK
UKHW021806220125
4208UKWH00049B/21

9 781805 667476